DON McCULLIN

HOUSTON PUBLIC LIBRARY

R01273 26121

Dew-pond, Somerset, 1988

Towards an Iron Age hill fort, Somerset, 1997

The Somerset Levels, near Glastonbury, 1994

The Somerset Levels, near Glastonbury, 1994

The Somerset Levels, near Glastonbury, 1994

DON McCULLIN

INTRODUCTION BY HAROLD EVANS
ESSAY BY SUSAN SONTAG

JONATHAN CAPE
LONDON

IN MEMORY OF THE SACRIFICE OF
DR ERICH SALOMON

12   INTRODUCTION BY HAROLD EVANS

16   ESSAY BY SUSAN SONTAG

18   THE BEGINNINGS

84   CYPRUS, 1964 AND 1965

98   THE CONGO, 1964 AND 1966

106 VIETNAM, 1965 AND 1968

138 BIAFRA, 1968–1970

152 THE HOMELESS, 1969

160 DERRY, 1971

172 CAMBODIA, 1970

180 BANGLADESH, 1971

194 CAMBODIA, 1975

200 BRADFORD AND THE NORTH, 1970s

216 BEIRUT, 1976 AND 1982

252 UPRIVER

286 BIOGRAPHICAL NOTES

288 BIBLIOGRAPHY

INTRODUCTION
Harold Evans

Don McCullin has the bottle. This is the man who amid a fusillade of bullets would stop to take a light reading. 'What's the point of getting killed if you've got the wrong exposure?' was the way he once put it to me. He risked his life so often that even the editors hungriest for his war photographs came to feel that this time, having survived the killing grounds of the Congo and Cyprus in the early sixties, and Israel's Six Day War in 1967, and then Vietnam and Biafra, he should be discouraged from going, say, to Cambodia in 1970, even forbidden to go to the Lebanon in 1976 or Afghanistan in 1980. Too many good photographers had died; Robert Capa and Larry Burrows had also seemed to lead charmed lives.

McCullin went anyway. It was Russian roulette. Fate's firing pin hit a bullet when he went out with a platoon of Cambodian soldiers in the rice swamps of Prey Veng. He was caught in a hail of automatic fire from the Khmer Rouge. He flung himself into the water, but kept his cameras on the ridge pointing to the attackers. One of his Nikons, he found later, had registered the perfect imprint of a round from an AK-47. He was exhilarated. He had escaped again. A couple of days later he heard that there was a firefight at Setbo and he was off once more, advancing along the Mekong River with Cambodian paratroopers. This time the spin of the chamber took him into another ambush. He was blasted backwards in a mortar barrage, hit by shrapnel four times in his right leg, once in the knee joint. He took his mind off the pain in his bleeding leg by photographing the rest of the wounded soldiers. Shortly after leaving hospital, he was back on the battlefield in Jordan. The devastating and poignant photographs of the Christian Falangist pogrom against the Palestinians in Beirut in 1976 were taken after he had been warned to desist on pain of death.

The stories from his lifetime of adventures are told with affecting candour in the autobiography he wrote with Lewis Chester, aptly entitled *Unreasonable Behaviour*; and in his book *Homecoming* he has written about his return to Britain from fourteen years of flying into danger. But there is something else about McCullin that is less well known than his bravery, something which this finely-presented collection should make as celebrated, and that is his artistry. Most of the photographs here have exciting or emotional stories attached to them, but many are distinguished, too, by composition, the compelling mood achieved by sombre lighting, and their sensitivity for the subjects. Leave aside for a moment the bloody detritus of foreign wars, and contemplate his rendering of an English country scene, fields in Somerset after a snow dusting. Nothing stirs. One's eye wanders the lonely landscape from an uninviting diagonal of leafless bushes to the folds in the landscape which climax in a black mound, an Iron Age hill fort. Dark scuds of clouds harass a watery sun. It is not calendar art. It is cold, and it is melancholy, and still it is serenely beautiful.

McCullin combines the elements with the brooding eye of a painter. The darkness of the printing is a trademark; in these landscapes he seeks to create a mood, but he avoids monotony by the variation in the light he admits and occasionally the placing of a figure. 'North of Glen Coe' is drama pushed to the limits of visibility, but compelling for all that; the infusion of light in the photograph on the Arafura Sea is hope yielding a moment in eternity.

Born in another time, raised in different circumstances, McCullin might have found his professional métier in drawing or sketching, perhaps not painting because he is partially colour-blind. I do not say this with regret, as an echo of the Photo-Secessionist insecurities about photography as art, but as a way of suggesting that McCullin's photographs bear contemplation because so often the documentary fact is expressed poetically. I have argued elsewhere* that the term 'decisive moment' should be reserved for those few photographs that offer both a story and a picture, that provide both a dramatic and a visual climax in the organic co-ordination of shapes, lines and values. The line of the Turkish boy's arm and hand reaching up to his mother on news of his father's death; the rushing gunman in overcoat preceded by his truncated shadow; the U.S. army medic comforting a wounded two-year-old; the sunlight lancing the darkened reception area of Beirut's shattered Holiday Inn, silhouetting a menacing figure under the chandeliers: how wrong it would be to crop the once-lavish environment.

Luck may come into decisive moments. The photograph of squaddies charging down a Bogside street would have been good without the housewife caught aghast, hand to her mouth. But McCullin was willing to be lucky; he has always been alert to the possibilities of composition and light. Coming on a father and two sons lying in their blood in a house in Cyprus, he writes, 'I felt as if I had a canvas in front of me and I was, stroke by stroke, applying the composition to a story that was telling itself. I was, I realised later, trying to photograph in a way that Goya painted or did his war sketches.' That may sound ingenuous; it is a good photograph but not a decisive moment. But McCullin is incapable of pretence. I saw his photograph of a shot Marine held on his feet by two buddies soon after it was taken during the Tet offensive, when McCullin spent eleven days in embattled Hue, but I had failed at the time to see correctly what McCullin does, that it resembles a painting of Christ being taken down from the cross. He does not mention it here, but I know that he helped to carry that wounded soldier to a first aid station.

It seems odd to say it of a man who has spent most of his life as a macho figure in combat gear, but McCullin is an aesthete. No trigger-happy paparazzo would have taken our imaginations into the ethereal mist of the Brontë vicarage and cemetery. Hardly any of us would have seen the romance in a couple going home in Finsbury Park on a wintry night or the fishermen playing football on the Scarborough beach. Only an aesthete with bare-knuckle determination could have cajoled the street gang, The Guvnors, into the theatrical poses in their best Sunday suits in the charred timbers of a bombed house. This was the photograph that got young Don McCullin his first assignment for the *Observer*. It is intriguing that he found inspiration in the back streets of Finsbury. How on earth did he do it? He, was one of the legion of working-class eleven-plus failures, resentfully saving up for his first Teddy Boy suit.

At Tollington Park Secondary Modern School someone noticed that he had a talent for drawing. It led to a trade art scholarship at the Hammersmith School of Arts and Crafts and Building, but at fourteen, on his beloved father's death, he had to give it up for a job as a pantry boy on a railway dining car in the days when the London, Midland and Scottish emblem meant something. It was a social and visual education. Travelling north for the first time in 1949 courtesy of LMS, he saw the two nations of post-war England. He absorbed perspective, watching the cities encroach, seeing the landscape slip by down in the valley and up high from the viaduct. He started seeing. He became a messenger in an animation studio, a promising opening that the Royal Air Force crowned in his national service days by assigning him a painter's job – painting numbers on thousands of film cans. And he failed the written test to be a photographer. Posted to Aden, his interest was maintained enough to forsake a pair of lionskin drums for a Rolleicord, which took his life's savings of £30, but when he was demobbed he pawned it for a quick fiver. If his mother had not generously insisted on spending everything she had to redeem 'that lovely camera', McCullin's life would have been different and we would have lost his memorable images.

His innate artistry, his courage and his proficiency with the camera are not a complete explanation of his achievements. Some of his images are reminiscent of other photographers. Robert Frank might have photographed the American car in Finsbury Park, Bill Brandt the sooty coal scavengers. But what strikes me most on seeing together pictures that were seen singly over years is the distinctive empathy of the photographer for the portraiture of people in his lens. It is there right from his early days photographing people in Finsbury Park against their wallpaper. He has not invaded their privacy; they are not his prey. He had involved them in the exercise. In Vietnam, he turned away from photographing a badly wounded man who waved him away. He just likes people as they are; he does not want to turn them into something else. You can see it in the way they look right into the lens: the man working in the iron foundry far from his native Bangladesh, the African father holding his starving child, the pigeon fancier in the north of England.

The portraits have a deceptive simplicity. They are sympathetic but not sentimental. They are not making any political points. The shell-shocked U.S. Marine in the battle for Hue in 1968 is treated exactly like the dazed bloodstained Vietnamese father blown out of his bunker by U.S. grenades. Perhaps they all know he feels their pride, their sorrow, their terror. He has known all their emotions. He is one of them in their common humanity, and that in the end is what marks McCullin, a person in search of something that is mysterious in his own life but profound in his pictures.

* Harold Evans, *Pictures on a Page*, 1978

WITNESSING
Susan Sontag

I have long admired Don McCullin's heroic journey through some of the most appalling zones of suffering in the last third of the twentieth century.

In a modern society, images made by cameras are the principal access to realities of which we have no direct experience. There have to be images, images of that kind, for something to become 'real'. For a war, an atrocity, a pandemic, a so-called natural disaster to become a subject of large concern, it has to reach people through the various systems (from television and the internet to newspapers and magazines) that diffuse photographic images to millions.

The upsetting photographs have the quality of being memorable – that is, unforgettable.

The photograph is like a quotation; or a maxim or proverb. Easy to retain. All of us mentally stock hundreds of photographic images, subject to instant recall. Cite the most famous photograph taken during the Spanish Civil War, Robert Capa's depiction of a Republican militiaman 'shot' by the camera just as he is shot by a bullet, and I wager that virtually everyone who has heard of that war can summon the grainy black-and-white figure at the top of a slope, arched backward with his arms outstretched, rifle in hand, at the very moment of death.

Photographs identify events. Photographs confer importance on events and make them memorable. We may understand through narrative but we remember through photographs, as David Rieff has written apropos of Ron Haviv's pictures of Serb-perpetrated atrocities and devastation in Bosnia between 1992 and 1996.

It seems unlikely that the earliest photographers of war – Roger Fenton, Alexander Gardner, Mathew Brady, Timothy O'Sullivan – meant to be protesting something when they photographed bodies on battlefields. But for nearly seventy years, that is, since the Spanish Civil War, when the main subjects of contemporary war photography were formulated, the leading practitioners of the photography of strife and of mass suffering – who are thought to be practising a form of journalism – have rarely considered themselves to be neutral or dispassionate observers.

In this great tradition of photojournalism, sometimes labelled 'concerned photography' or 'the photography of conscience', no one has surpassed – in breadth, in directness, in intimacy, in unforgettability – the gut-wrenching work produced by Don McCullin.

There can be no doubt of the intentions of this tenacious, impassioned witness, bringing back his news from hell. He wants to sadden. He means to arouse.

It has become a cliché in the discussion of such images to assert that they no longer have the impact they once had. Michael Ignatieff has written that 'war photography – thanks to television – has now become a nightly banality. We are flooded with images of atrocity.' This 'nightly barrage of images of atrocity' risks deadening our 'delicate human capacity to transmute aesthetic vision into moral insight'.

What would such critics of the voracious appetite of the mass media for strong sensations actually recommend? Is it that, for the sake of slowing down the banalization of evil, images of atrocity be confined to a weekly barrage? Is it what I myself called for in *On Photography*: an 'ecology of images'? But there *isn't* going to be an ecology of images. No Committee of Guardians is going to ration our exposure to the almost-unbearable-to-look-at, to keep fresh its ability to shock. And the horrors themselves are not going to abate either.

I would suggest that it is a good in itself to acknowledge, to have enlarged, one's sense of how much suffering there is in the world we share with others. I would insist that anyone who is perennially surprised that depravity exists, who continues to experience disillusionment (even incredulity) when confronted with evidence of what humans are capable of inflicting in the way of gruesome, hands-on cruelties upon other humans, has not reached moral or psychological adulthood.

No one after a certain age has the right to this kind of innocence, of superficiality, to this degree of ignorance, of amnesia.

We now have a vast repository of images that make it harder to preserve such moral defectiveness. Let the atrocious images haunt us. Even if they are only tokens and cannot possibly encompass all the reality of a people's agony, they still perform an immensely positive function. The image says: keep these events in your memory.

The fact that we are not totally transformed, that we can turn away, turn the page, switch the channel, does not impugn the ethical value of such images. It is not a defect, either in McCullin's photographs themselves or in the system used here to deliver them, a handsome book, that we don't suffer *enough* when we look at them.

We actually understand very little by just looking at the photographic witness of some heartbreaking arena of indignity, pain, and death. Seeing reality in the form of an image cannot be more than an invitation to pay attention, to reflect, to learn, to examine the rationalizations for mass suffering offered by established powers.

There are questions to be asked. Who caused what the picture shows? Who is responsible? Is it excusable? Was it inevitable? Is there some state of affairs which we've accepted up to now that ought to be challenged?

A photograph can't coerce. It won't do the moral work for us. But it can start us on the way.

THE BEGINNINGS

Young Teddy Boy, McCullin's youth club, church hall, Finsbury Park, London, 1961

Sheep going to slaughter, early morning,
near the Caledonian Road, London, 1965

Finsbury Park, London, 1961

Near the Caledonian Road, London, 1960

In the café with the gang, London, 1958

American car belonging to a boxer, Fonthill Road, Finsbury Park, London, 1963

The Guvnors in their Sunday suits, Finsbury Park, London, 1958

Berlin, 1961

West Berliners looking east, 1961

East German guard, Berlin Wall, 1961

American and East German border guards, Friedrichstrasse crossing, Berlin, 1961

High alert, Friedrichstrasse crossing, Berlin, 1961

Near Checkpoint Charlie, Berlin, 1961

West Berliners, Sunday afternoon, the Wall, 1961

Checkpoint Charlie, Berlin, 1961

Friedrichstrasse, Berlin, 1961

American troops looking across the Wall, Berlin, 1961

Outside Buckingham Palace, 1960

Hessel Street, Jewish district, East End, London, 1962

Chapel Market, Islington, London, 1959

Sunday morning, Chapel Market, Islington, London, 1962

Sunday morning, Chapel Market, Islington, London, 1962

Near Hornsey Road, London, 1958

Chapel Market, Islington, London, 1962

Liverpool 8, early 1960s

Gypsy watching the police evict his family, Kent, early 1960s

The Brontë graveyard, Haworth, Yorkshire, 1960s

Crowther's Reclamation Yard, Isleworth, 1960

The Death Collector, Holloway Road, London, mid-1960s

Aldgate, London, 1961

Early morning, west Hartlepool, County Durham, 1963

Early morning, west Hartlepool, County Durham, 1963

Coal miners leaving their shift, Doncaster, Yorkshire, 1967

Unemployed men gathering coal from the shore,
west Hartlepool, County Durham, 1963

Unemployed men gathering coal, Sunderland, early 1970s

Coal searchers, Sunderland, early 1970s

Late winter sun, Scarborough, Yorkshire, 1967

Fishermen playing during their lunch break, Scarborough, Yorkshire, 1967

A schoolboy who has lost his parents, the wedding of Princess Alexandra, the Mall, London, 1963

Protester, Cuban missile crisis, Whitehall, London, 1963

Anti-fascist demonstration, Hackney, London, 1963

Anti-fascist demonstration, at National Socialist Party rally, Trafalgar Square, London, 1962

Anti-fascist demonstration, at National Socialist Party rally, Trafalgar Square, London, 1962

Skinheads, Southend, 1980s

Southend, 1980s

Chicago jail, 1967

Prisoner asking for water, Chicago jail, 1967

Liberation fighters assembling to disarm after victory, Rhodesia, 1979

Young boy at an assembly point after being press-ganged into the army, southern Sudan, 1991

Family group, father with Russian machine-gun, southern Sudan, 1991

Tibetan refugees at the railway station, Delhi, 1965

Nomadic tribespeople working on a farm, central India, 1965

CYPRUS, 1964 AND 1965

Turkish inhabitants awaiting Greek attack, Limassol, Cyprus, 1964

Turkish defender leaving the side-entrance of a cinema, Limassol, Cyprus, 1964

Turks retrieving the body of an old man killed by a Greek sniper, under the protection of a British armoured car, Limassol, Cyprus, 1964

Turkish woman discovering the body of her new husband, killed with his brother and father, Cyprus, 1964

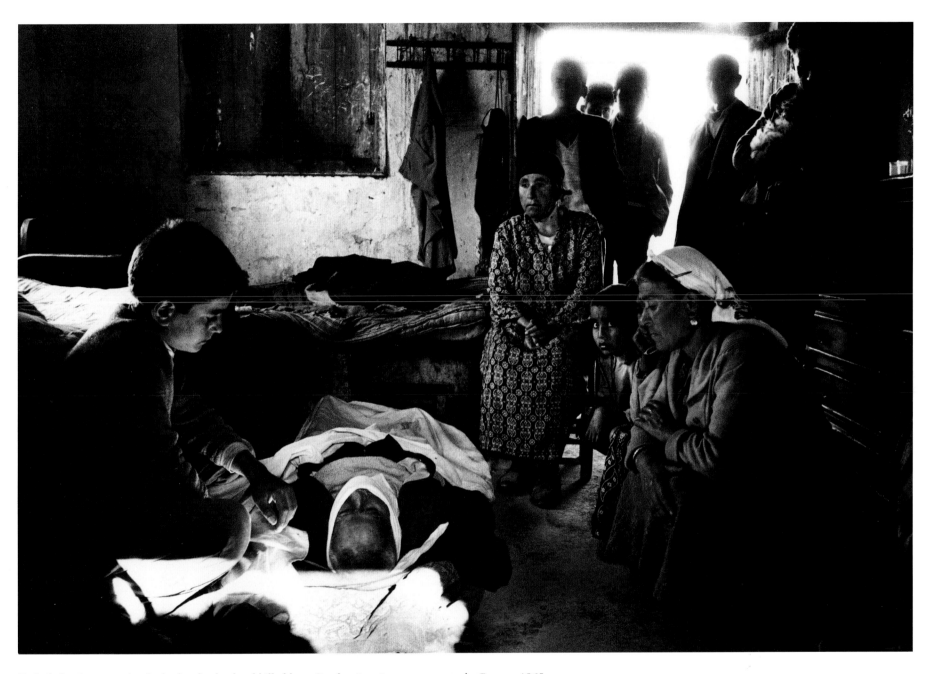

Turkish family mourn by the body of a shepherd killed by a Greek sniper in a revenge attack, Cyprus, 1965

Turkish woman by her husband's body, Cyprus, 1964

Turkish woman grieving for her dead husband, Cyprus, 1964

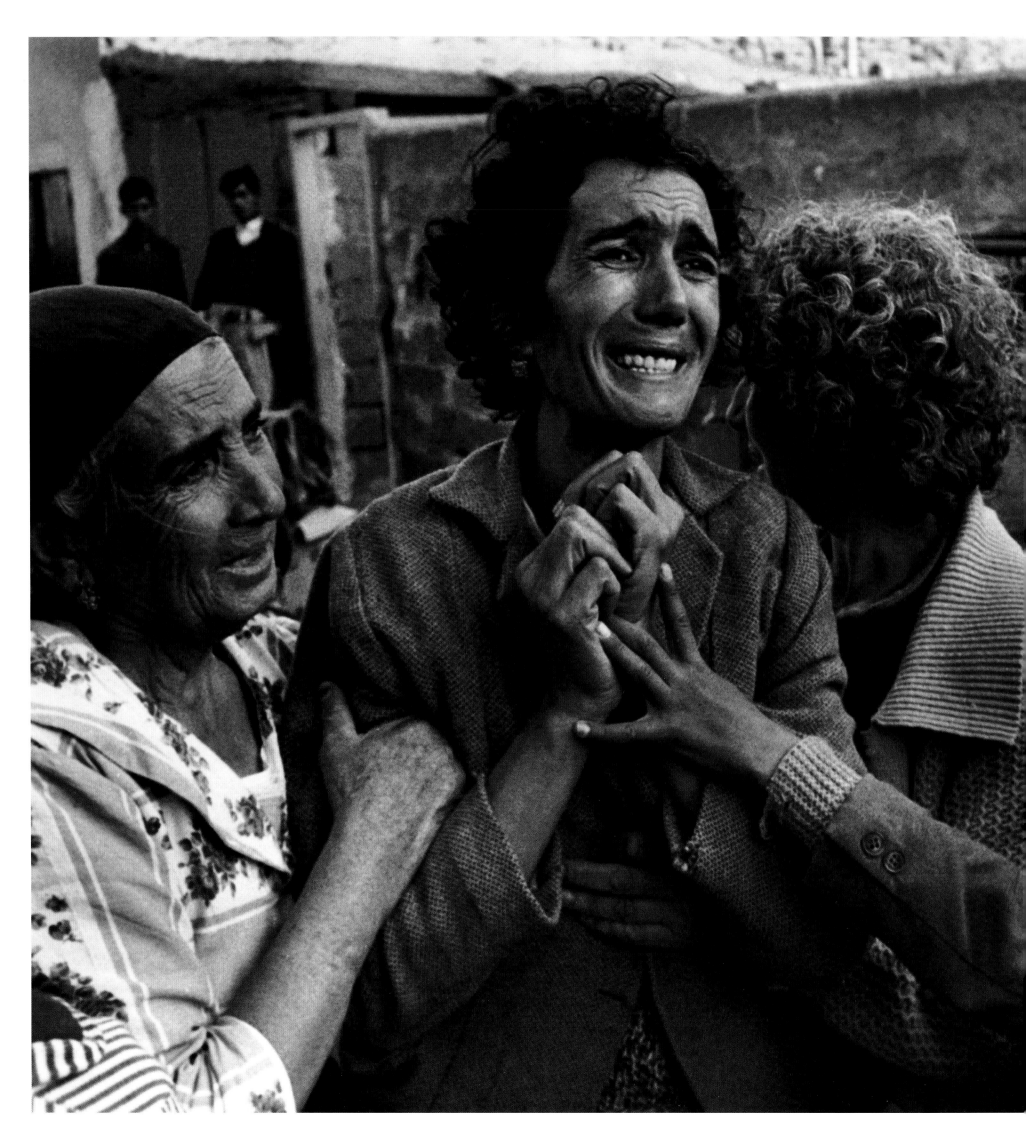

Turkish woman mourning the death of her husband, Cyprus, 1964

Cyprus, 1964

THE CONGO, 1964 AND 1966

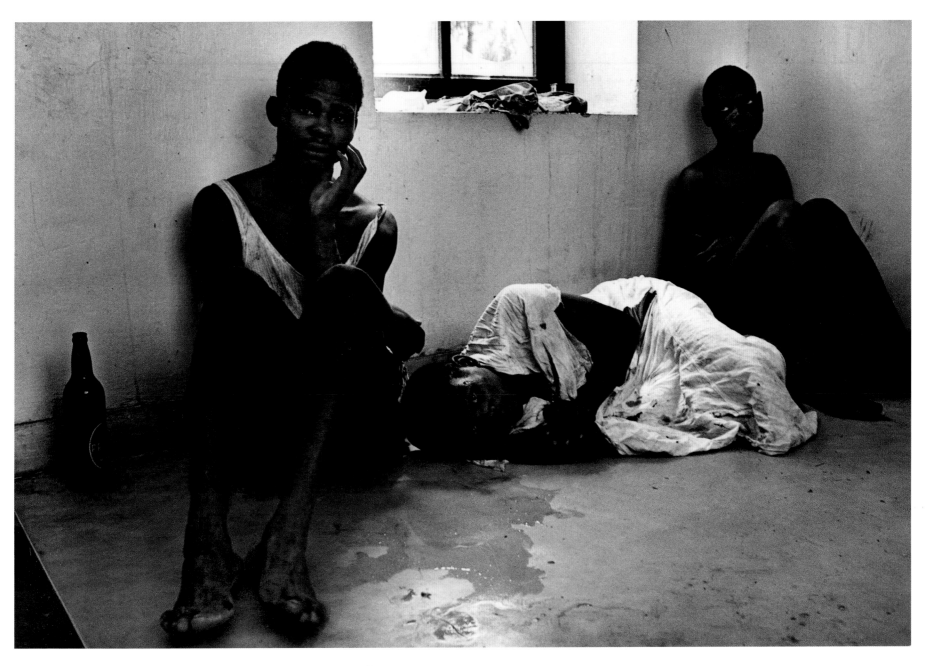

Suspected Lumumbist freedom fighters await their fate in jail, Stanleyville, 1964

Suspected Lumumbist freedom fighters being
tormented before execution, Stanleyville, 1964

White mercenary and Congolese family, Paulis, north of Stanleyville, 1966

Murdered man, shot through the brain, Stanleyville, 1964

VIETNAM, 1965 AND 1968

Shell-shocked U.S. Marine, Hue, 1968

Mekong Delta, 1965

Mekong Delta, 1965

Viet Cong suspect and South Vietnamese troops, Mekong Delta, 1965

Viet Cong suspect being dragged from his bunker, Mekong Delta, 1965

Viet Cong suspect, Mekong Delta, 1965

The Citadel, Hue, 1968

The Citadel, Hue, 1968

U.S. Marine caught in sniper fire, the Citadel, Hue, 1968

Wounded U.S. officer, the Citadel, Hue, 1968

The Citadel, Hue, 1968

The Citadel, Hue, 1968

U.S. Marines, the Citadel, Hue, 1968

U.S. army chaplain rescuing Vietnamese woman, Hue, 1968

Wounded North Vietnamese soldier retrieved from his bunker by U.S. Marines, Hue, 1968

Dying U.S. Marine carried by tank through
the ruins of the Citadel, Hue, 1968

U.S. Marine hurling a grenade seconds before
being shot through the left hand, Hue, 1968

U.S. Marine sniper, a nineteen-year-old from Scotland, Hue, 1968

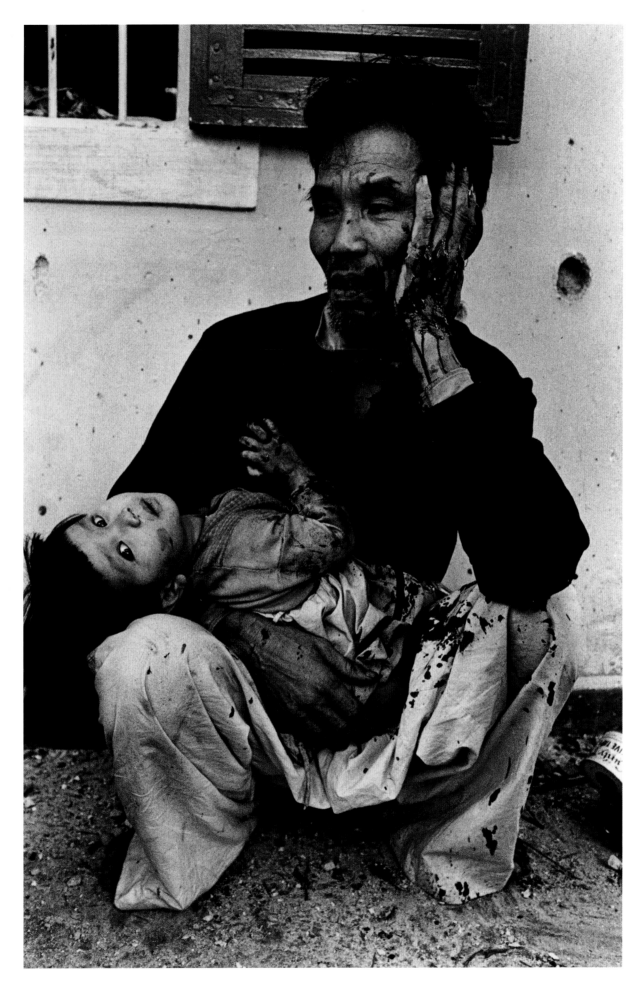

Father and daughter after a grenade-attack on their bunker, Hue, 1968

A civilian tormented by U.S. Marines as a Viet Cong suspect before his release, Hue, 1968

U.S. Marine medic rushing a wounded two-year-old child from the battle, Hue, 1968

Vietnamese family after a grenade-attack on their bunker, Hue, 1968

A captured Viet Cong suspect before his release, Hue, 1968

A dead North Vietnamese soldier and his plundered belongings, Hue, 1968

The body of a North Vietnamese soldier, Hue, 1968

The body of a North Vietnamese soldier, Hue, 1968

BIAFRA, 1968–1970

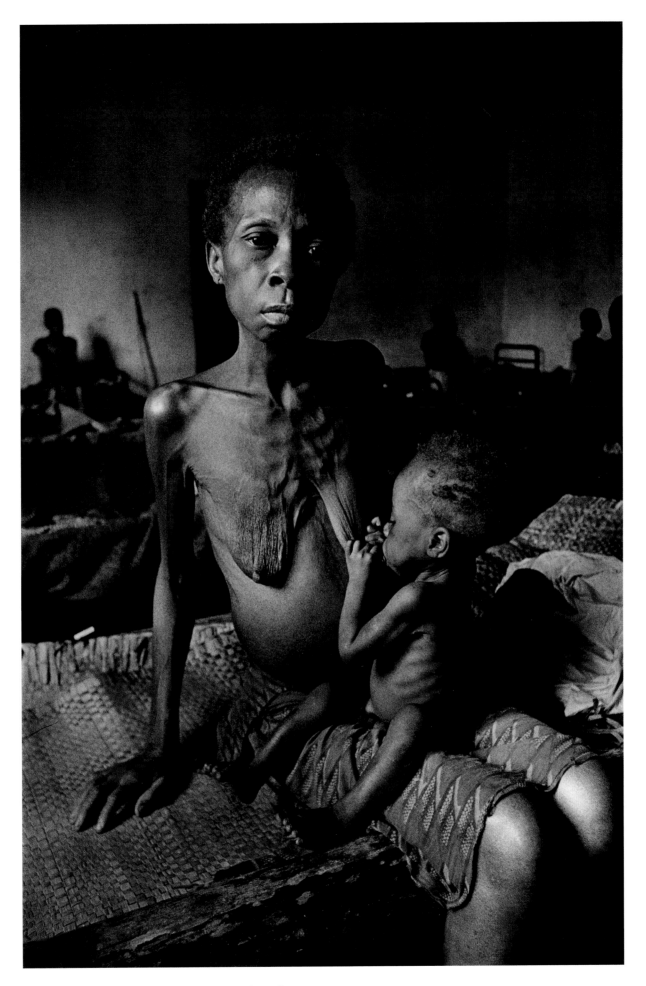

A 24-year-old mother and child awaiting death, Biafra, 1968

Escaping from the front line, Biafra, 1968

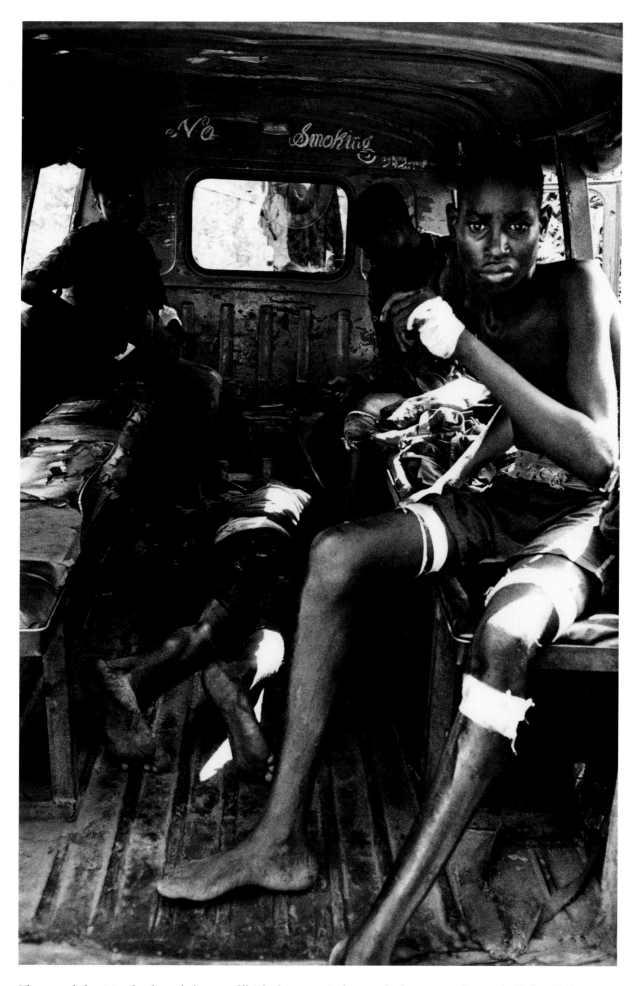

The wounded waiting for the ambulance to fill. The lying man is about to die from stomach wounds. Biafra, 1968

A Biafran officer addressing one of his dead soldiers, 1968

A grievously wounded soldier attended by a medic who has no morphine, Biafra, 1968

Biafran soldiers awaiting food, 1968

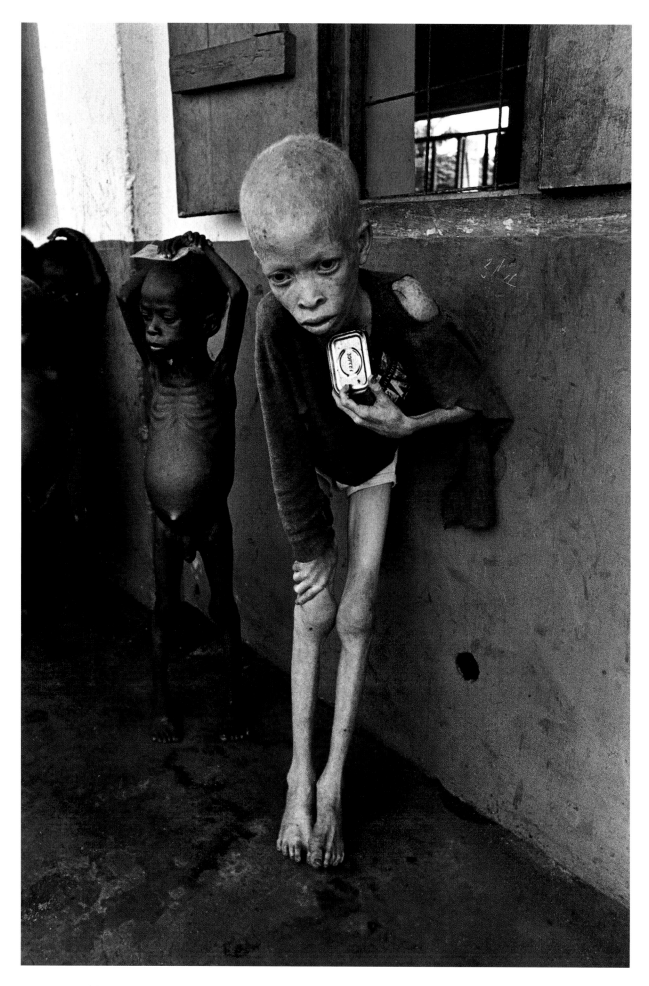

A nine-year-old albino boy clutching an empty corned beef tin, Biafra, 1968

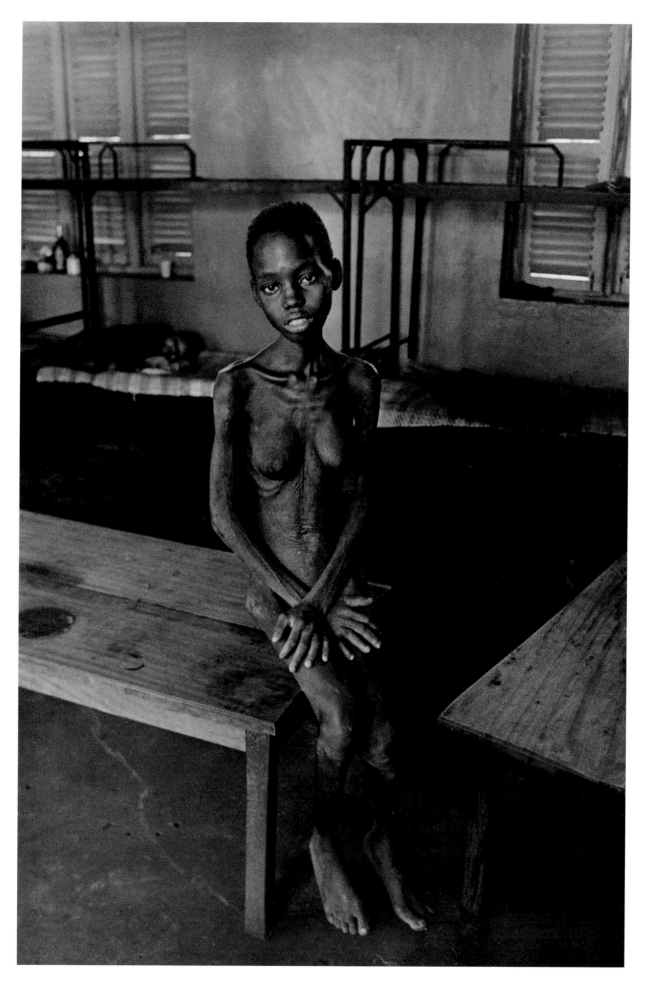

A sixteen-year-old girl called Patience, Biafra, 1968

A mother and some of her children waiting for a
food hand-out which will never arrive, Biafra, 1968

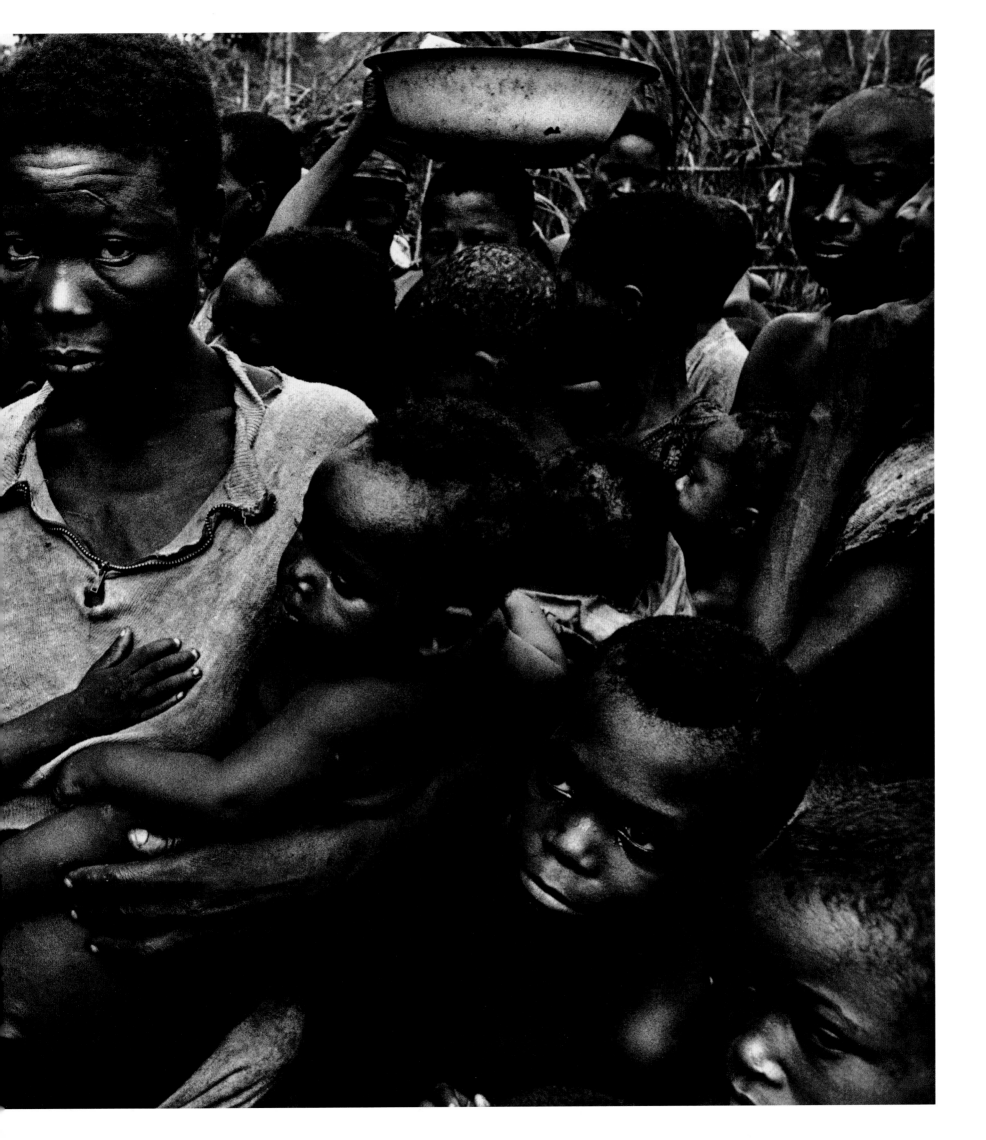

Waiting for food, Biafra, 1970

A sixteen-year-old mentally handicapped boy. The doctor laughed at him. Biafra, 1968

THE HOMELESS, 1969

Aldgate, London, 1969

Homeless and mentally disturbed woman, Aldgate, London, 1969

Homeless and mentally disturbed Irishman, Aldgate, London, 1969

In the shadow of Hawksmoor's Christ Church, Spitalfields, London, 1969

Scavenging in the East End, London, 1969

Tormented, homeless Irishman, Spitalfields, London, 1969

DERRY, 1971

A sergeant hit by a brick, the Bogside, Derry, 1971

The Bogside, Derry, 1971

The Bogside, Derry, 1971

Racist abuse being hurled at a black soldier by a woman above, while a Catholic rioter is arrested, the Bogside, Derry, 1971

Youths taunting British soldiers who are firing CS gas, the Bogside, Derry, 1971

Catholic youths escaping from CS gas, Derry, 1971

Jubilant stone-thrower, the Bogside, Derry, 1971

CAMBODIA, 1970

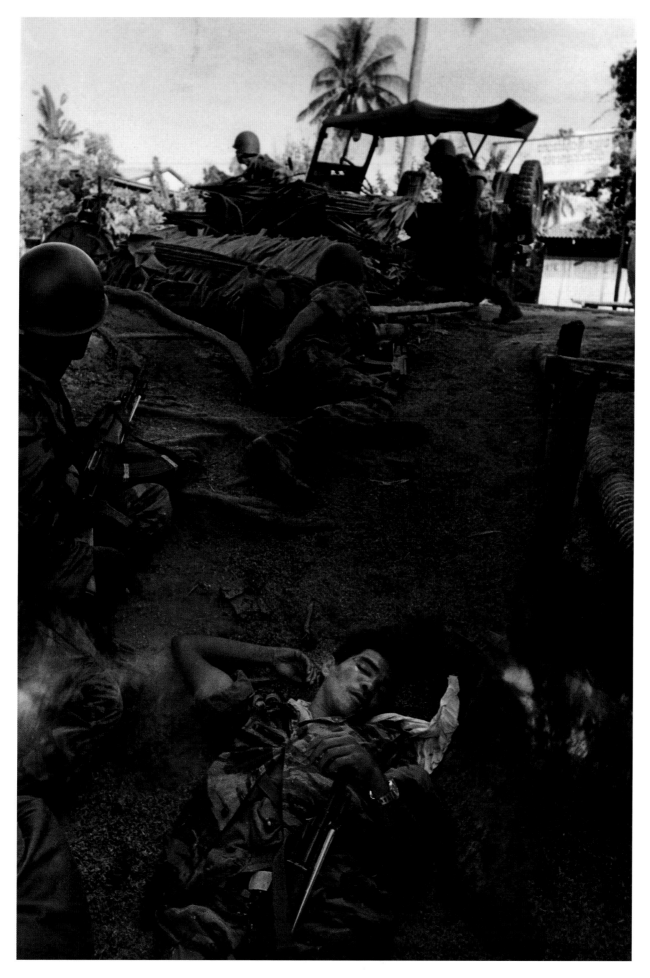

Moments before McCullin is hit by fragments of an 82mm mortar shell, Cambodia, 1970

Dying Cambodian paratrooper hit by the same
mortar shell that hit McCullin, Cambodia, 1970

Cambodia, 1970

Two dead Khmer Rouge, one with a missing foot possibly as a result of a landmine, Prey Veng, Cambodia, 1970

BANGLADESH, 1971

Refugees, Bangladesh, 1971

The monsoon season on the Indian border with Bangladesh, 1971

Refugees at an assembly point, where 10,000 arrived
daily, some showing signs of cholera, Bangladesh, 1971

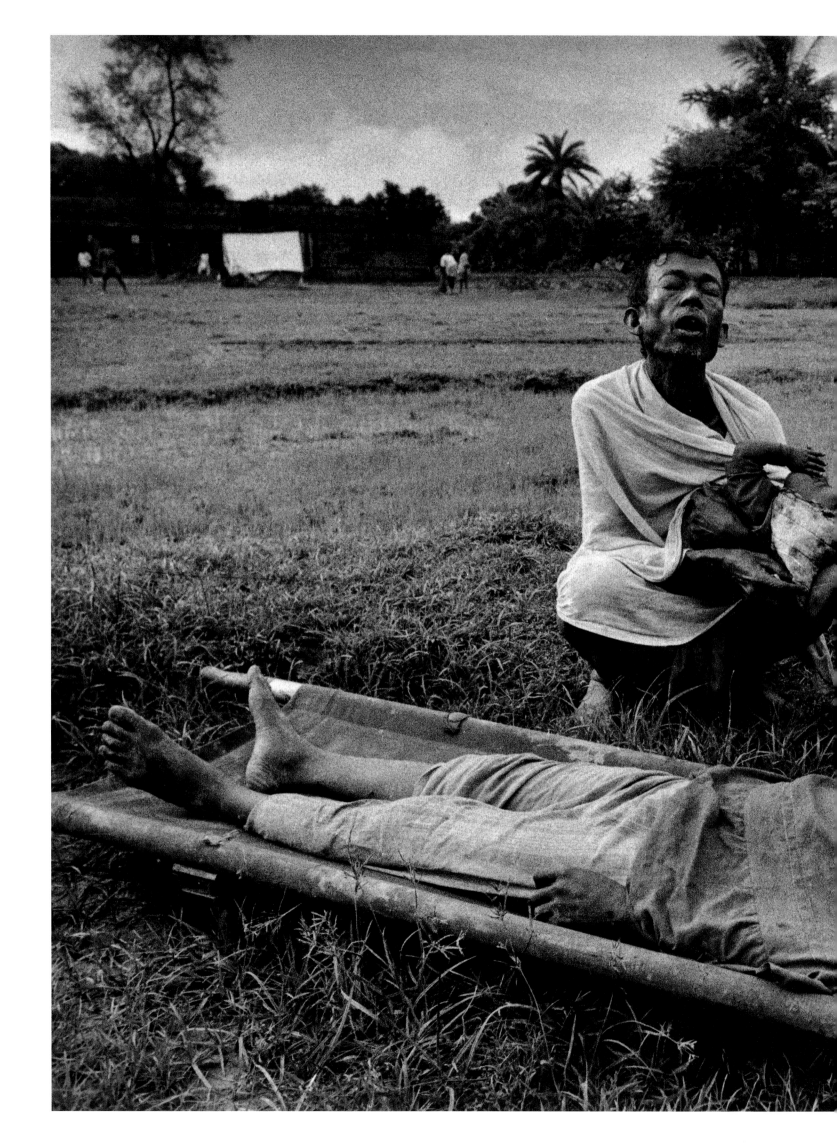

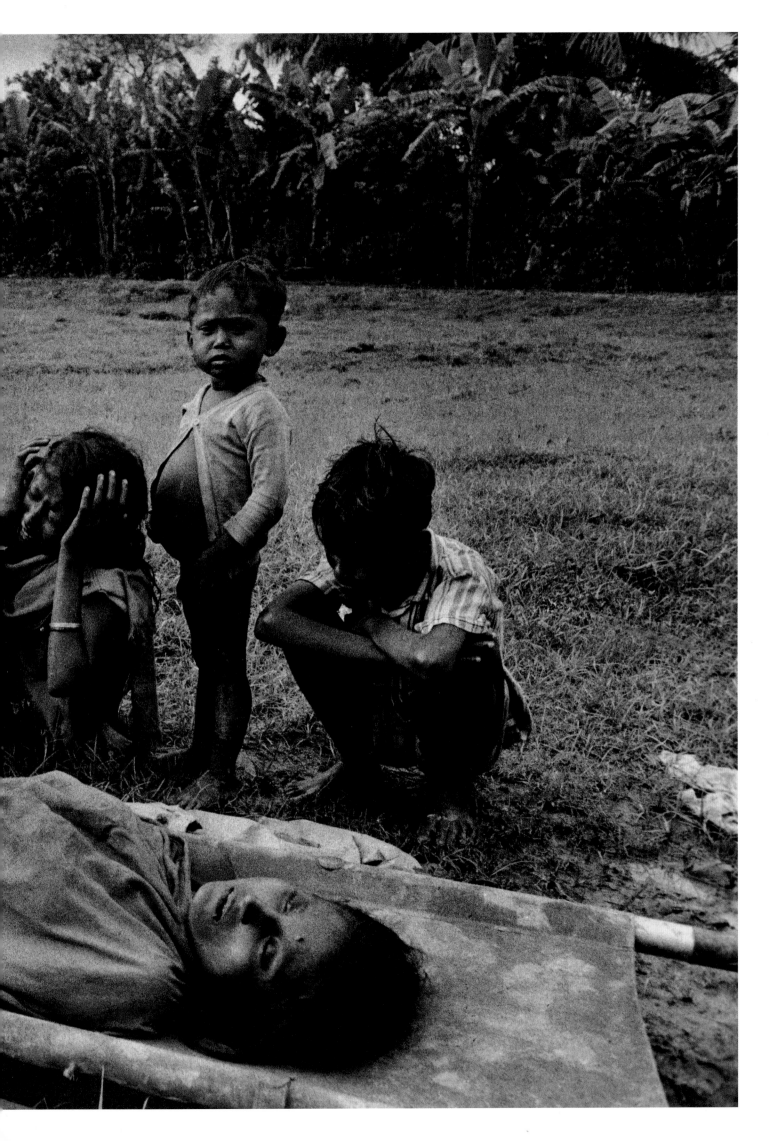

A grieving husband and family with
the body of their mother, on the
Indian border, Bangladesh, 1971

187

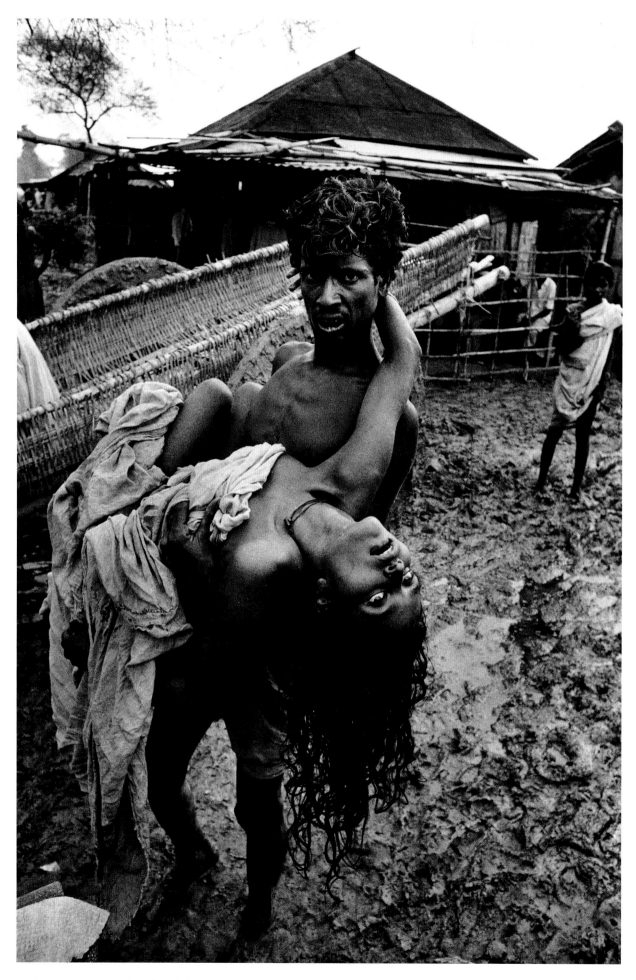

A cholera victim, Bangladesh, 1971

Contaminated water cooling a cholera victim, Bangladesh, 1971

A mother separated from her husband stands over her child, sick with cholera, Bangladesh, 1971

A father holding the body of his nine-year-old son, Bangladesh, 1971

A young woman recovering from cholera in a flooded school serving as a hospital, Bangladesh, 1971

Helpless father and sick child, Bangladesh, 1971

CAMBODIA, 1975

A madhouse after the guards have deserted, Phnom Penh, 1975

The inside of an overflowing hospital, Phnom Penh, 1975

The main hospital, Phnom Penh. The wounded soldier would have been killed subsequently by the Khmer Rouge. 1975

Landmine victim, Phnom Penh, 1975

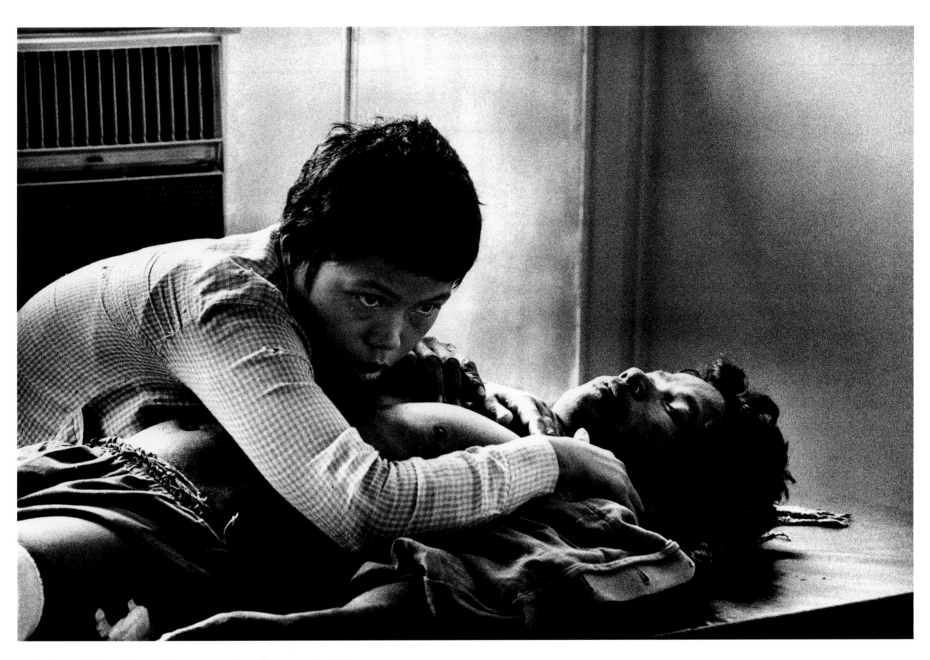

A dead Cambodian soldier and grieving widow, Phnom Penh, 1975

BRADFORD AND THE NORTH, 1970s

A steel-worker with his pigeons, Consett, County Durham, 1974

Bradford, 1978

Consett, County Durham, 1974

Consett, County Durham, 1974

Asian worker, the Bingley Iron Foundry, Bradford, 1978

Bradford, 1978

Man and two sons, one of whom has lost a leg in a scrapyard accident, Bradford, 1978

Bradford, 1978

Meal time for the children, cooked on a camping stove (their father is in prison), Bradford, 1978

Miss Wade, Bradford, 1978

Woman posing in her best clothes, Bradford, 1978

BEIRUT, 1976 AND 1982

Christian woman with grenade, Holiday Inn, Beirut, 1976

Palestinians in training, Beirut, 1976

Christian gunmen in the foyer of the Holiday Inn, battling
with Palestinians in the adjacent hotel, Beirut, 1976

Christian gunmen leading away Palestinian women and
children before they murder their menfolk, Karantina,
East Beirut, 1976

Palestinian men over the age of fourteen rounded up by Christian gunmen. Within hours they were all murdered and their bodies burned. Karantina, East Beirut, 1976

Old Palestinian and his wife begging for mercy from the Christian gunmen, Beirut, 1976

Looters and corpse, Beirut, 1976

Christian gunmen mocking a Palestinian couple
who have been spared the slaughter, Beirut, 1976

Women and children fleeing an impending
massacre, Karantina, East Beirut, 1976

Old man killed in crossfire, Karantina, East Beirut, 1976

McCullin was ordered by the Christians under threat of death
to leave the area when he came across the young Christians
beside the body of a teenage Palestinian girl. Beirut, 1976

Child in a mental hospital which has been shelled, Sabra, Beirut, 1982

Child tied to a bed in a mental hospital which was under Israeli shellfire for five days, Sabra, Beirut, 1982

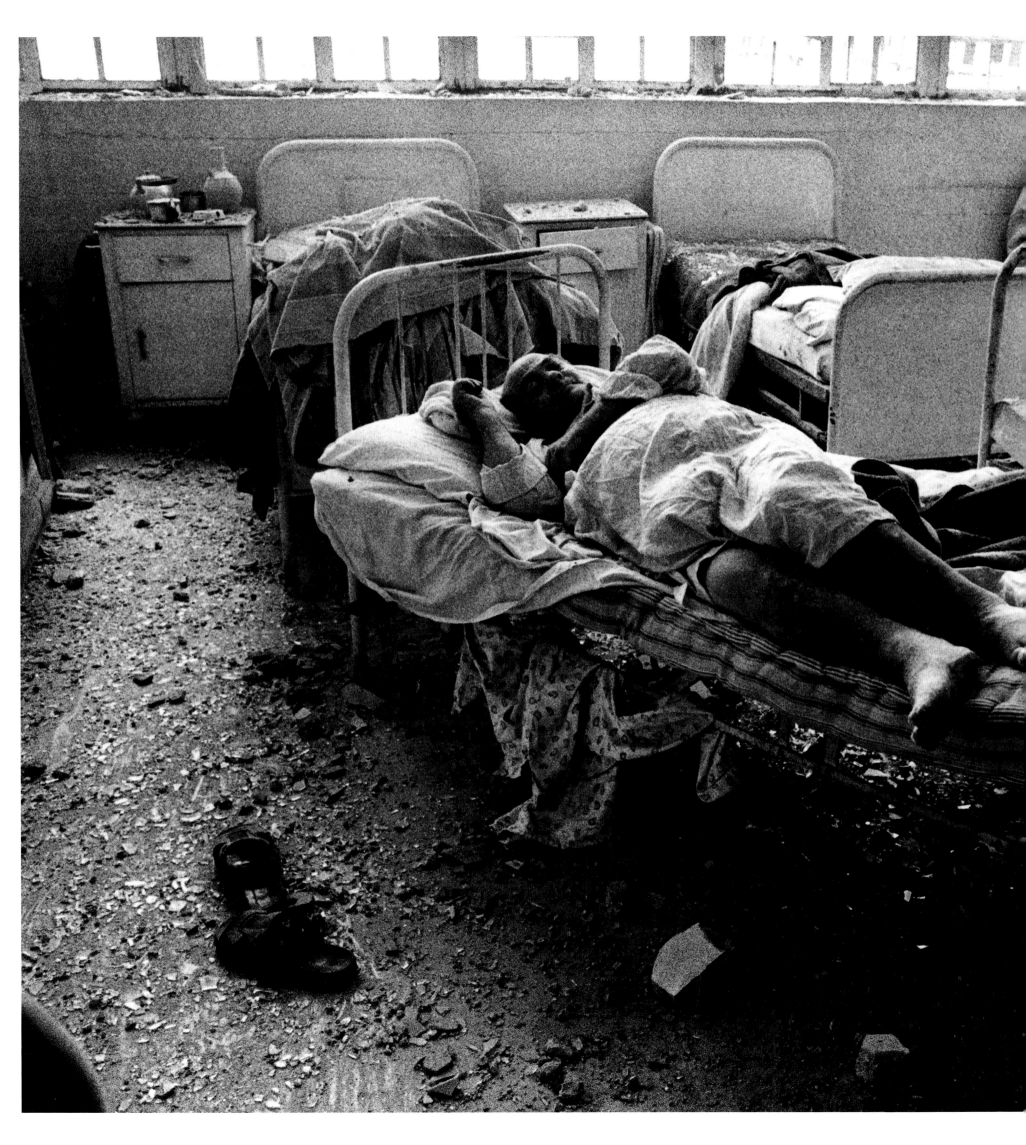

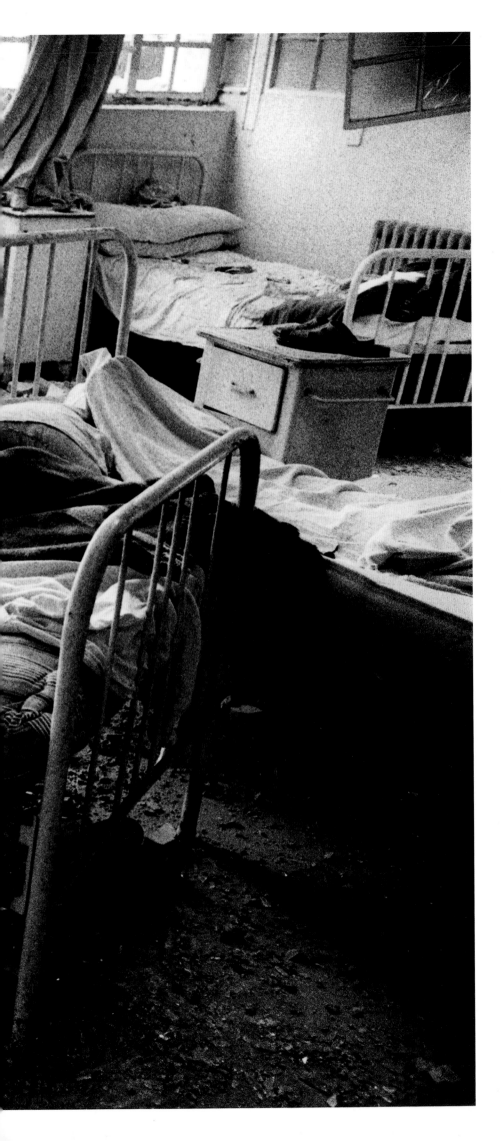

Hospital shelled by Israelis, Sabra, Beirut, 1982

The inhabitants of a mental hospital moving each other after shelling, Sabra, Beirut, 1982

Mental hospital after shelling, Sabra, Beirut, 1982

DATE DUE

IFARW   779
          .092
          M478

MCCULLIN, DON
   DON MCCULLIN

IFARW   779
          .092
          M478

HOUSTON PUBLIC LIBRARY
CENTRAL LIBRARY

7/10

Man by the ruins of his house, shelled for
days by Israeli tanks and ships, Beirut, 1982

A Palestinian woman returning to the
ruins of her house, Sabra, Beirut, 1982

A Palestinian woman asking why her family has been massacred, Sabra, Beirut, 1982

A Palestinian family leaving the
Martyr's Cemetry, Beirut, 1976

UPRIVER

The Ganges at dusk, Patna, India, 1998

The elephant festival, Sonepur Mela, on the Gandak river near Patna, India, 1989

Pilgrims bathing at the Gandak river at dawn, near Patna, India, 1989

Beggar at the holy festival, Sagar Island, at the junction of the Ganges and the Brahmaputra rivers, India, 1997

Early morning at the Kumbh Mela, Allahabad, India, 1989

Festival of the sea gods, Bali, 1984

Fishermen returning from the Arafura Sea, Agats, Irian Jaya, 1985

Irian Jaya, 1985

Village chief, with ballpoint pen through his nose, who claimed to be a cannibal, Irian Jaya, 1992

Hill tribesmen practise archery after a pig feast, Irian Jaya, 1992

A chief whose village was under threat from the logging industry, Siberut, Mentawai Islands, sixty miles from the coast of Sumatra, 1984

Near Agats, Irian Jaya, 1992

Boat festival, Siberut, Mentawai Islands, sixty miles from the coast of Sumatra, 1984

Irian Jaya, 1992

Ochenep, Irian Jaya, 1985

Cannibals, Wortu, Irian Jaya, 1985

Tribeswoman and child from a remote region of Irian Jaya, 1985

A man of the forest, Irian Jaya, 1985

Blind woman, Ochenep, Irian Jaya, 1985

Women, from the Stone Age, Buepis, Irian Jaya, 1985

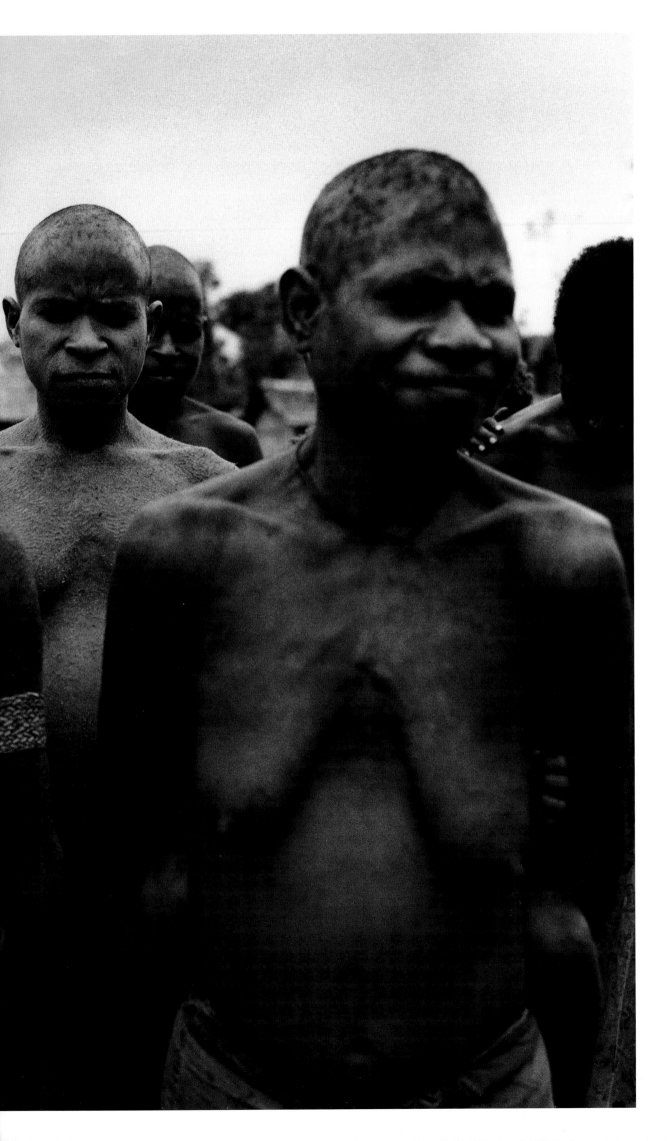

Last descendants of a vanishing tribe who have been persuaded to cut their hair and stop tattooing, in keeping with modern times, Siberut, the Mentawai Islands, 1986

Siberut, the Mentawai Islands, 1986

Ceremonial gathering, Irian Jaya, 1992

A man and his three wives returning from a funeral. The woman is covered in ashes as a sign of respect. Irian Jaya, 1992

A pig feast, Irian Jaya, 1992

Irian Jaya, 1992

Before a feast, Irian Jaya, 1992

Men returning to their village and stopping
for water after a pig feast, Irian Jaya, 1992

BIOGRAPHICAL NOTES

1935   Born in London. His father was an invalid. The family lived off Tottenham Court Road, in King's Cross, and then in Finsbury Park.

1940   Evacuated to Somerset.

1946   Failed the eleven-plus examination and went to Tollington Park Secondary Modern School.

1949   Won a trade art scholarship to the Hammersmith School of Arts and Crafts and Buildings. His father died, aged forty, and he was forced to find work to earn money for the family. He became a pantry boy on the London, Midland and Scottish Railway dining cars, travelling between London and Manchester.

1950   Worked as a messenger boy for W. M. Larkins, a cartoon animation studio, in Mayfair.

1954   Called for national service and joined the R.A.F. Posted to the Canal Zone in Suez where he became a photo assistant. This was followed by postings in Kenya and Cyprus. Acquired his first camera, a Rolleicord, which he later pawned for £5.

1959   One of his acquaintances from a north London gang, The Guvnors, was tried for the murder of a policeman and executed. Brought his photographs of The Guvnors to the *Observer* and his first work was published.

1961   Flew to Berlin, without an assignment, to photograph the building of the Wall. Won a British press award.

1964   Received his first international assignment for the *Observer*, to photograph the war in Cyprus, for which he received the World Press Photo Award. Awarded the Warsaw Gold Medal. Sent to the Congo to cover the rebellion by supporters of the murdered President Lumumba. Entered Stanleyville disguised as a mercenary.

1965   Dispatched by the *Illustrated London News* to Vietnam.

1966   Joined the *Sunday Times Magazine* where he stayed for eighteen years.

1967   Arrived in Jerusalem during the Six Day War.

1968   Arrived in Vietnam and covered the fighting around the Citadel in Hue during the Tet Offensive. Later in the year he photographed in Czechoslovakia, Biafra and Cuba. He also photographed the Beatles.

1969   His assignments included documenting the genocide of the Brazilian Indians.

1970   Photographed in New Guinea. Wounded in Cambodia.

1971   Photographed the refugees in Bangladesh, victims of floods and cholera.

1974   Photographed the steel works in Consett, County Durham.

1975   Worked in Phnom Penh, Cambodia, before the fall of the city to the Khmer Rouge.

1976   Photographed the civil war in Beirut.

1977   Awarded a Fellowship of the Royal Photographic Society.

1980   First major retrospective exhibition, at the Victoria and Albert Museum, London.

1984   First visited the Mentawai Islands off the coast of Sumatra to photograph the isolated tribespeople with his younger son, Alexander, and Mark Shand. He returned the following year to photograph in Irian Jaya.

1993   Awarded a C.B.E. Received an Honorary Doctorate from the University of Bradford. Given the Dr Erich Salomon Award in Germany.

1994   Awarded an Honorary Degree by the Open University.

1999   Received a Kaiser Foundation Award to photograph the victims of AIDS in Africa.

2000   AIDS photographs exhibited at the Whitechapel Art Gallery in London and at the United Nations in New York.

Don McCullin by Nick Wheeler, with Delta Company, 1st Battalion of the 5th Marines, the Citadel, Hue, 1968

BIBLIOGRAPHY

The Destruction Business, London, 1971

Is Anybody Taking Any Notice?, Cambridge, Massachusetts, 1971

Homecoming, London, 1979

The Palestinians, with Jonathan Dimbleby, London, 1979

Hearts of Darkness, Introduction by John Le Carré, London, 1980

Beirut: A City in Crisis, London, 1983

Perspectives, London, 1987

Skulduggery, with Mark Shand, London, 1987

Open Skies, Introduction by John Fowles, London, 1989

Unreasonable Behaviour: An Autobiography, London, 1990

Sleeping with Ghosts, Introduction by Mark Haworth-Booth, London, 1994

India, Introduction by Norman Lewis, London, 1999

Iraqi tank shell exploding on a Kurdish position, on the road to Arbile, northern Iraq, 1991

Loch Tulla, Scotland, 1992

North of Glen Coe, Scotland, 1992

The battlefields of the Somme, France, 2000

Dew-pond by Iron Age hill fort, Somerset, 1988

Published by Jonathan Cape 2001

1 3 5 7 9 10 8 6 4 2

Photographs copyright Don McCullin © 2001
Introduction copyright Harold Evans © 2001
Essay copyright Susan Sontag © 2001
Photograph of Don McCullin by Nick Wheeler, Hue, 1968 © Nick Wheeler

Don McCullin has asserted his right under the Copyright, Designs
and Patents Act 1988 to be identified as the author of this work

This book is sold subject to the condition that it shall not, by way of trade
or otherwise, be lent, resold, hired out, or otherwise circulated without the
publisher's prior consent in any form of binding or cover other than that in
which it is published and without a similar condition including this condition
being imposed on the subsequent purchaser

First published in Great Britain in 2001 by Jonathan Cape, Random House,
20 Vauxhall Bridge Road, London SW1V 2SA

The Random House Group Limited Reg. No. 954009
www.randomhouse.co.uk

A CIP catalogue record for this book is available from the British Library

ISBN 0-224-06133-X

Editor: Mark Holborn
Designed by Mark Holborn with Antigone Konstantinidou
Text Editor: Tristan Jones
Production Director: Neil Bradford
Printed in Italy by Conti Tipocolor, Florence